CW00666757

Skipping Games

Energetic Workouts for Lively Children
by Jenny Mosley & Helen Sonnet
pictures by Mark Cripps

Positive Press ✓

How to use this book

The skipping activities in this book are set out beginning with the easiest games first and becoming progressively more challenging. If you have a group or individuals who are unable to skip, many of the activities can be done with a rope swung gently to and fro. You will need different lengths of rope for individual, small- and large-group skipping. It is a good idea to begin the game giving each child an opportunity to skip and to practice rope turning while another child skips. Make sure the children turn the rope towards the entering skipper. As the children become more proficient, you can increase their skill level by introducing the following more advanced skipping techniques.

The skipping beats and instructions appear below the rhymes. The instructions throughout this book are given as a guide and can be used to encourage children, as well as the teachers, to read and initiate the games themselves.

Abbreviations

↘S - child jumps 'in'

S↗ - child jumps 'out'

S - one skip

Ⓐ - swing the rope gently from side to side

Ⓑ - swing the rope in a full circle

①②③ - indicates child ① child ② and so on, when there are a number of children skipping in the group at the same time

Skipping Games rules...how to play happily together

All games start with a pair of children who volunteer to swing the rope. The whole group take it in turns to skip or turn the rope

In all the rhymes the group of children join in the chant. The group wait patiently until it is their turn to 'skip in'. If the child trips or catches the rope the chant is resumed without forfeit.

Skipping Styles

Where style Ⓐ or Ⓑ is not indicated on a rhyme in this book, you should choose the style that suits the confidence of the group. Both styles can be used on ALL games.

Style Ⓐ

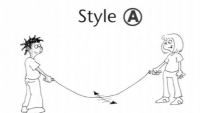

Good for beginners -
the rope is swinging to and fro

Style Ⓑ

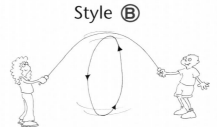

Good for the more confident skippers -
the rope is swung in a full circle

Try these fun skipping challenges

- Increasing the speed of the rope
- Moving forward whilst skipping
- Crossed arms skipping
- Skip forward then backward
- Turning the rope twice while jumping
- Use two ropes for ground skipping

Printed by: Heron Press, 19-24 White Hays North, West Wilts Trading Estate, Westbury, Wiltshire BA13 4JT

Published in 2004 by: Positive Press Ltd,
28A Gloucester Road, Trowbridge, Wiltshire BA14 OAA

Text copyright© Jenny Mosley & Helen Sonnet
Illustrations copyright© Mark Cripps

ISBN 095454 1154

Skipping Games

Is skipping an endangered skill among children? Well, that is a distinct possibility! Soon there may be nobody left to pass on the spectacular techniques that previous generations learned on the playground. Our own children, we were dismayed to discover, were unable to skip at all, let alone skip with the skill that used to be so widespread.

This lapse is a pity because skipping has now become a competitive sport. The British Rope Skipping Association holds competitions at both the national and international level and there is even talk of skipping being accepted as an Olympic sport. Boys, particularly, might be surprised to discover the stamina and skills required for skipping, or 'plyometrics' as it is called by athletes, which improves cardio-respiratory fitness, flexibility and coordination.   All these benefits have been recognised by the British Heart Foundation, who organised the first 'Jump Rope For Heart' in 2002. As Hazel Mackie, the event organiser, puts it: "As well as being a great deal of fun, skipping has many health, educational and social benefits."

Skipping requires practice to master but the synthesis of action and concentration becomes easier as we progress, and as the sense of achievement grows, so does the motivation to continue. The complexity of the movements stimulates whole brain functioning, requiring both sides of the brain to work together, thus heightening cognitive function and making the brain work better. Skipping is fun and it's free – when you come right down to it, all you need is a length of rope.

Skipping is also a very sociable activity. When skipping with groups, it's a good idea to assemble various lengths of rope – shorter for individual skipping, mid-length for two or three skippers and one or two long ropes for large skipping groups. Begin each lesson with some individual skipping to get participants in the right frame of mind and warmed up. Before you start the games, routinely remind everyone that the rope must turn towards the one who is about to enter the game. With a group of beginners, we suggest starting with the rope swinging gently to and fro and progress to rope turning as their skills develop.

The skipping activities in this book are designed in just that way – to proceed from the simple to truly impressive displays of magnificent agility. They have catchy chants that bring rhythm, humour, exercise, accomplishment and companionship to your playground, making it a happy place full of those who spend their free time doing something that has been enjoyed since rope was invented – and that was a very long time ago! You will find both traditional and modern chants in this book. You could even create some of your own.

So ... get that rope moving, leap joyfully over it, sing together, get fit and, most importantly, have fun.

Helen Sonnet

Jenny Mosley
*(Member of the Q.C.A. PE and
School Sports (PESS) Steering Committee)*

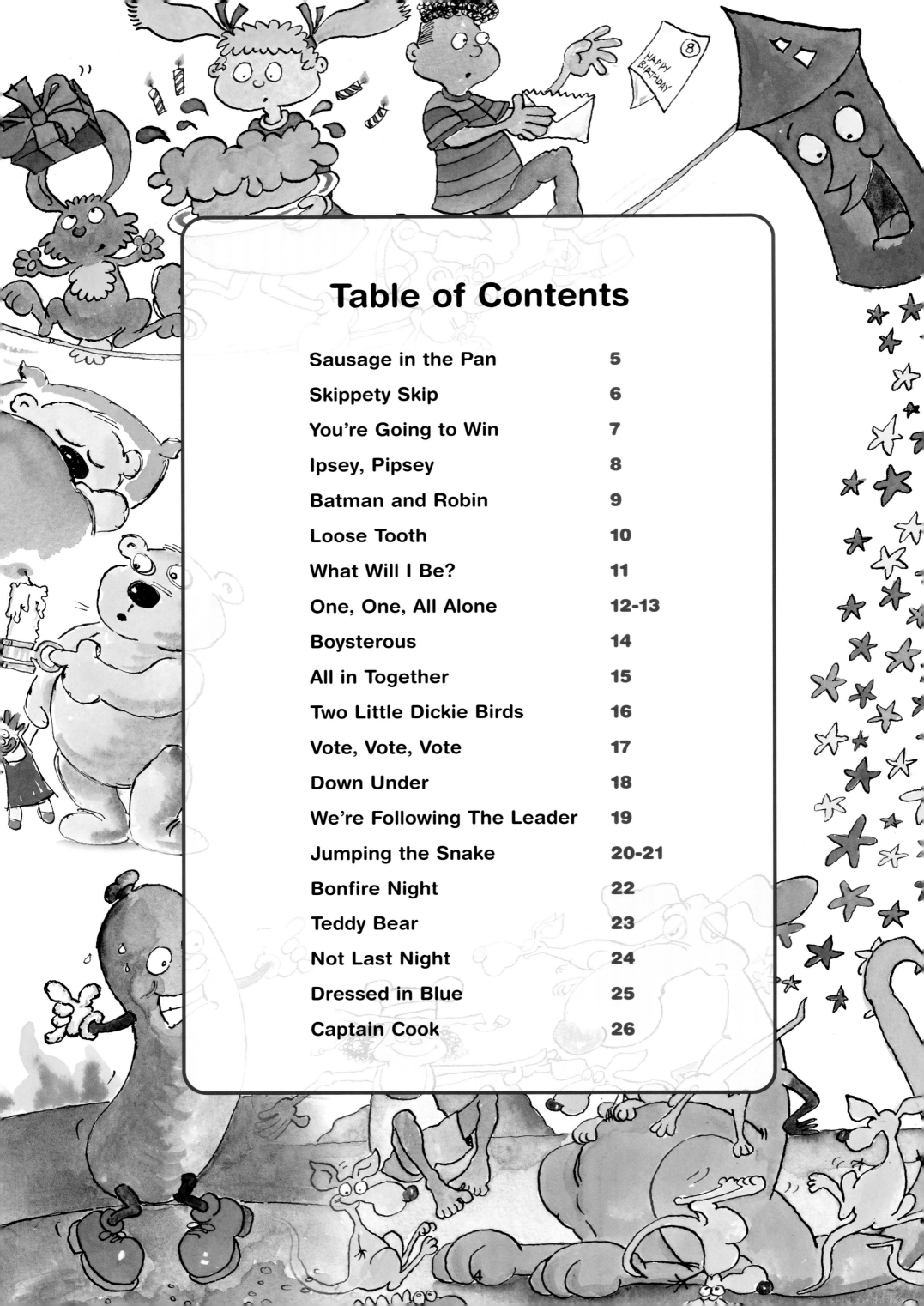

Table of Contents

Sausage in the Pan

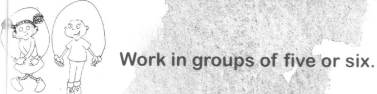

Work in groups of five or six.

Sausage in the pan

↘S   S

Ⓐ |— swing the rope gently from side to side —|

Sausage in the pan

S   S

Ⓐ |— swing the rope gently from side to side —|

Turn it over

S

Ⓑ |— swing the rope in full circle —|

Turn it over

S

Ⓑ |— swing the rope in full circle —|

Sausage in the pan.

S   S↗

Ⓐ |— swing the rope gently from side to side —|

If you feel confident, increase the number of 'sausages in the pan' by having two or more children skip together.

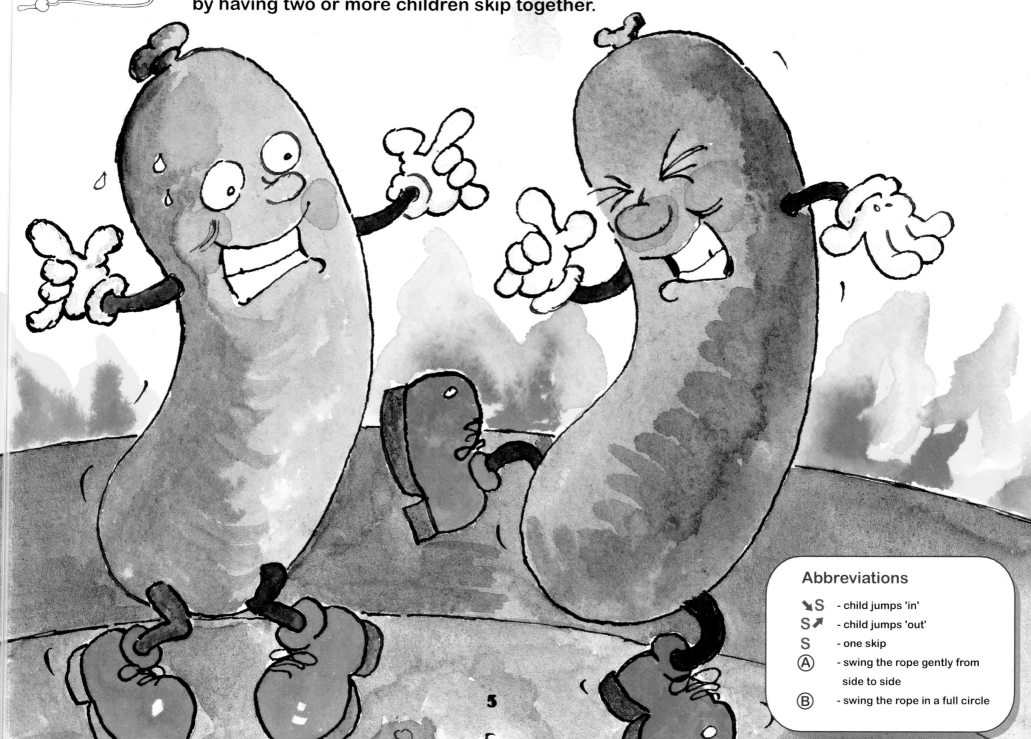

Abbreviations

↘S - child jumps 'in'

S↗ - child jumps 'out'

S - one skip

Ⓐ - swing the rope gently from side to side

Ⓑ - swing the rope in a full circle

Skippety Skip

Work in groups of five or six.

Skippety skip
S   S

Hoppity hop
S   S

Snickety snick
S   S

Clippety clop
S   S

Trickety track
S   S

Jiggedy jog
S   S

Clickety clack
S   S

Diggedy dog.
S   S

 The purpose of the game is to say interesting
sounding words and the children can make up their own as well.

You're Going to Win

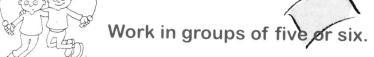

Work in groups of five or six.

You're going to win the lot-ter-y
　　　S　　　　S　　　　S　　　S

And be as rich as you can be.
S　　　S　　　S　　　S

How many pounds will you get?
S　　　　S　　　S　　　S

One, two, three, four, five, six, etc.
S　　S　　S　　S　　S　　S

Ⓑ ———————— swing the rope gradually faster ————————

Each child skips until they are out on the final count.

Abbreviations

↘S - child jumps 'in'

S↗ - child jumps 'out'

S - one skip

Ⓐ - swing the rope gently from side to side

Ⓑ - swing the rope in a full circle

Ipsey, Pipsey

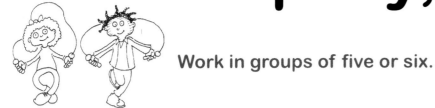

Work in groups of five or six.

Ipsey, pipsey tell me true

↘S   S   S   S

Who shall I be married to?

S   S   S   S

A, B, C, D, E, F, etc. (continue chanting alphabet)

S S S S S S

when the skipper trips, he/she has to think of someone's name beginning with that letter

If you think that the words of this traditional rhyme are inappropriate, you can change them to:

Ipsey, pipsey don't you tease
Tell me who my friend is please.
A, B, C, D, E, F, etc.

Batman and Robin

Work in groups of five to ten. Children can either skip individually or several children can skip together.

Batman and Robin went to town
↘S   S   S   S

Batman wore his dressing gown.
S   S   S   S

How many colas did they down?
S   S   S   S

One, two three, four, five, etc.
S   S   S   S   S

|— the rope is turned or swung faster and counting continues until the rope is stopped —|

You could use this rhyme as a competition to see who can reach the highest count.

Abbreviations
↘S   - child jumps 'in'

S↗   - child jumps 'out'

S   - one skip

Ⓐ   - swing the rope gently from side to side

Ⓑ   - swing the rope in a full circle

Loose Tooth

Work in groups of five or six.

I've a loose tooth, a loose tooth in my mouth
↘S   S   S   S

It's wiggly and jiggly and pointing to the south.
    S   S   S   S

Ow, ouch, eeee, ow, ouch
S   S   S   S

I want it out to put it in my pouch.
    S   S   S   S

When, oh when, oh when will it come out?
    S   S   S   S

I scream and cry and yell and shout.
    S   S   S   S

MONDAY, TUESDAY, WEDNESDAY,
    S   S   S
|— the rope is turned or swung faster until the child stops the rope —|
THURSDAY, FRIDAY, SATURDAY, SUNDAY.
    S   S   S   S
|— the rope is turned or swung faster until the child stops the rope —|

if the child skips beyond
Sunday, begin the week again.

What Will I Be?

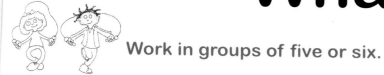

Work in groups of five or six.

What will I be when I leave school?
↘S   S   S   S

Rich or poor, wise or a fool?
S   S   S   S

Plain or fancy, bad or good?
S   S   S   S

Tell me now, if you would.
S   S   S   S

Tinker, tailor, soldier, sailor, rich man, poor man, beggar man, thief.
S   S   S   S   S   S   S   S

Ⓑ |——— turn the rope faster and faster until the rope is stopped by the child ———|

Abbreviations

↘S - child jumps 'in'

S↗ - child jumps 'out'

S - one skip

Ⓐ - swing the rope gently from side to side

Ⓑ - swing the rope in a full circle

One, One, All Alone

Work in groups of ten to fifteen with a long rope.

One, one, all alone, feeling sad and blue

S   S   S   S   S   S   S   S

first child jumps in

Calls in --------------- and then there were two.

S   S   S   S   S   S   S   S

second child jumps in

Two, two, having fun, happy as can be

S   S   S   S   S   S   S   S

Call in --------------- and then there were three.

S   S   S   S   S   S   S

third child jumps in

Three, three, friends together, want even more

S   S   S   S   S   S   S   S

Call in -------------- and then there were four.

S   S   S   S   S   S   S   S

fourth child jumps in

Four, four, skip some more, it's good to be alive

S   S   S   S   S   S   S   S

The activity begins with one child skipping who calls in a friend. The second child calls in the third, the third child calls in the fourth and so on. At the end, each child jumps out one at a time.

Call in -------------- and then there are five.

S   S   S   ↘S   S   S   S   S

fifth child jumps in

Five, five, it's very full, squashed as close as bricks

S   S   S   S   S   S   S   S   S

Call in -------------- and then there are six.

S   S   S   ↘S   S   S   S   S

sixth child jumps in

Six, six is enough, each with a friend

S   S   S   S   S   S   S   S

Now jump out one by one and that will be the end.

S   S   S   S   S   S   S

One----two----three-----four-----five----six.

S↗ S↗ S↗ S↗ S↗ S↗

1st one jumps out   2nd child jumps out   3rd child jumps out   4th child jumps out   5th child jumps out   6th child jumps out

13

Boysterous

Work in groups of five or six. This activity has been included especially for the boys.

RUN, RUN, RUN, RUN, RUN
↘S   S   S   S   S

Ⓑ |———— jump from one foot to the other ————|

JUMP, JUMP, JUMP, JUMP, JUMP
S   S   S   S   S

Ⓑ |———— jump with feet together ————|

HOP, HOP, HOP, HOP, HOP
S   S   S   S   S

Ⓑ |———— hop on one foot ————|

DOWN, DOWN, DOWN, DOWN, DOWN
S   S   S   S   S↗

Ⓑ |———— jump crouching down low ————|

The object is to approach the rope on the move and continue the action through or over the rope without hesitation. If a child hesitates or stops the rope he or she is out. When they have gone through the actions once, they repeat them with the rope turning faster. They continue in this manner until there is a winner.

All in Together

Work in groups of eight to ten with a long rope.

All in together girls (boys)

⊢————— the rope turners chant —————⊣

This fine weather girls (boys)

⊢————— the rope turners chant —————⊣

When you hear your birthday

⊢————— the rope turners chant —————⊣

Please jump in:

⊢——— the rope turners chant ———⊣

January, February, March, April

↘S   ↘S   ↘S   ↘S

⊢——— the children jump in and skip when their birthday month is called ———⊣

May, June, July, August,

↘S   ↘S   ↘S   ↘S

⊢——— the children jump in and skip when their birthday month is called ———⊣

September, October, November, December.

↘S   ↘S   ↘S   ↘S

⊢——— the children jump in and skip when their birthday month is called until all ———⊣
the children are skipping together

If there are mixed gender groups they can say 'friends'. The rope turners then repeat the chant asking the skippers to jump out when their birthday month is called. The children take turns to turn the rope or skip.

Abbreviations

↘S - child jumps 'in'

S↗ - child jumps 'out'

S   - one skip

Ⓐ   - swing the rope gently from side to side

Ⓑ   - swing the rope in a full circle

Two Little Dickie Birds

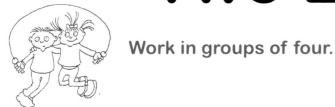

Work in groups of four.

Two little dickie birds sitting on a wall

Peter - ↘S   S   S   S

Paul - ↘S   S   S   S

One called Peter and one called Paul

Peter - S   S   S   S

Paul - S   S   S   S

Fly away Peter, fly away Paul

Peter - S   S↗

Paul - S   S   S   S↗

Come back Peter, come back Paul.

Peter -   ↘S   S   S

Paul -   ↘S

Take turns to be two 'dickie birds' or rope turners. The birds decide who is Peter and who is Paul. They start skipping while the rope turners chant the first two lines. On the third line, they jump out of the rope, first Peter and then Paul, and return on the next line when their name is called.

16

Vote, Vote, Vote

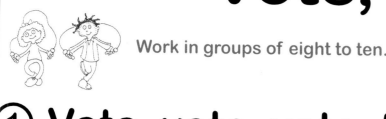 Work in groups of eight to ten.

① **Vote, vote, vote, for** (name of child one) _____ _____

child one - ↘S   S   S   S

② **Calling in** (name of child two) _____ **at the door**

child one - S   S   S   S

child two - ↘S   S   S

③ (name of child two) _____ **is the one and we want a bit of fun**

child one - S   S   S   S

child two - S   S   S   S

④ **so we won't vote for** (name of child one) _____ **anymore**

child one - S   S   S   S

child two - S   S   S   S

⑤ **CHUCK HER(HIM) OUT!**

child one - S↗

child two - S

Rope turners say the chant, inserting the first name and surname of a child into the first line. A second child then jumps in and skips together with the first child. In the fourth line, the rope turners say just the first name of the original skipper who jumps out in line five. The process is repeated until all the children have been called in to skip.

Down Under

Work in groups of ten to fifteen with a long rope.

Down under in the outback

child one -   S   S

├──── child one is chosen to start the skipping ────┤

Jumped a kangaroo. Out popped a joey

child one -   S   S   S   S

And jumped in too.

child one -   S   S
child two -   S

How many more joeys can jump in?

child one -   S   S   S   S
child two -   S   S   S   S

One, two, three, four, five, six, seven, etc.

↘S   ↘S   ↘S   ↘S   ↘S   ↘S   ↘S

When the rope has been stopped count how many 'joeys' there are. The object is to try and get more and more children skipping together.

18

We're Following The Leader

Work in groups of eight to ten.

1. We're following the leader, the leader, the leader.

(E) |———————— swing the rope in a full circle towards the children ————————|

We're following the leader, wherever he(she) may go.

(B) |———————— swing the rope in a full circle towards the children ————————|

2. We're going through the tunnel, the tunnel, the tunnel.

(B) |———— the rope is swung in a full circle and each child takes their turn to run under the ————|
rope before it touches the ground

We're going through the tunnel, and out the other side.

(B) |———— the rope is swung in a full circle and each child takes their turn to run under the ————|
rope before it touches the ground

3. We're going 'cross the ocean, the ocean, the ocean.

(A) |———— swing the rope gently from side to side and each child takes their turn to jump ————|
over it and out the other side

We're going 'cross the ocean to see the U.S.A.

(A) |———— swing the rope gently from side to side and each child takes their turn to jump ————|
over it and out the other side

Verse 1: The children form a line and each child in turn, jumps in, skips twice and jumps out the other side, returning to the back of the line.

Verse 2: The children take turns to run under the rope before it touches the ground.

Verse 3: The rope is swung to and fro and the children take turns to jump over it and out the other side.

Abbreviations	
↘S	- child jumps 'in'
S↗	- child jumps 'out'
S	- one skip
(A)	- swing the rope gently from side to side
(B)	- swing the rope in a full circle

19

Jumping the Snake

 Work in groups of four to six.

1. Jumping over the slithery snake

|———— shake the rope low on the ground ————|

Forwards, backwards, forwards, backwards.

|———— shake the rope low on the ground ————|

Hiss, hiss, snake in the grass

|———— shake the rope low on the ground ————|

Backwards, forwards, backwards, forwards.

|———— shake the rope low on the ground ————|

2. Marching down to Buckingham Palace

Ⓐ |———— swing the rope gently from side to side ————|

Right, left, right, left.

Ⓐ |——— swing the rope gently from side to side ———|

Facing forward, smart and ready

Ⓐ ┠── swing the rope gently from side to side and each child takes their ──┨ turn to hop over the rope

Left, right, left, right.

Ⓐ ┠── swing the rope gently from side to side and each child takes their ──┨ turn to hop over the rope

3. Leaping over the giant waves

↘S   S   S   S

Ⓑ ┠──────── swing the rope in a full circle ────────┨

Over, over, over, over.

S   S   S

Ⓑ ┠──── swing the rope in a full circle ────┨

Splash, splash, laugh and shout

S   S   S   S

Ⓑ ┠──────── swing the rope in a full circle ────────┨

Over, over, then jump out.

S   S   S↗

Ⓑ ┠──────── swing the rope in a full circle ────────┨

Verse 1: The rope is shaken low on the ground and the children jump over it with both feet together on lines 2 and 4.
Verse 2: The rope is gently swung to and fro. The children hop over it on right or left feet.
Verse 3: The rope is turned and the children skip, jumping out on the last line.

Abbreviations

↘S   - child jumps 'in'

S↗   - child jumps 'out'

S   - one skip

Ⓐ   - swing the rope gently from side to side

Ⓑ   - swing the rope in a full circle

Bonfire Night

Work in groups of five or six.

Bonfire night, bonfire night

S   S   S   S

Jumping jacks, what a fright!

S   S   S   S

— child does star jump —

Catherine wheels turn around

S   S   S   S

— child turns around —

Screamers flash on the ground.

S   S   S   S

— child touches ground —

Rockets fly into the sky

S   S   S   S

— child puts arms by side —

From the ground, way up high.

S   S   S   S

— child jumps as high as they can —

Wave your sparklers, having fun

S   S   S   S

— child mimes waving sparkler —

Crackling bonfire, your turn's done.

S   S   S   S

child jumps out

All the children chant as the child skips.

Teddy Bear

Work in groups of five or six.

Teddy bear, teddy bear turn around
↘S   S   S   S
|— turn around —|

Teddy bear, teddy bear touch the ground
S   S   S   S
|— touch the ground —|

Teddy bear, teddy bear climb the stairs
S   S   S   S
|— mime climbing stairs —|

Teddy bear, teddy bear say your prayers
S   S   S   S
|— place your hands together —|
in a prayer

Teddy bear, teddy bear turn off the light
S   S   S   S
|— mime switching off light —|

Teddy bear, teddy bear say Good Night.
S   S   S   S↗
|— shout 'Good Night' and jump out —|

The children perform or mime the actions as they are chanted.

Abbreviations

↘S   - child jumps 'in'
S↗   - child jumps 'out'
S   - one skip
(A)   - swing the rope gently from side to side
(B)   - swing the rope in a full circle

23

Not Last Night

Work in groups of four to six.

Not last night, but the night before
S   S   S   S

Twenty four robbers came knocking at my door.
S   S   S   S

They called me out, they called me in
S   S   S   S

They told me how I had to begin.
S   S   S   S

"Spanish dancer turn around,
S   S   S   S
|—— turn around ——|

Spanish dancer touch the ground.
S   S   S   S
|—— touch the ground ——|

Spanish dancer do the kicks,
S   S   S   S
|—— kick the air ——|

Spanish dancer do the splits!"
S   S   S   S
|—— jump over and ——|
     with legs astride
     stop the rope

The children skip one at
a time and follow the instructions.
Boys can substitute the words
'Ninja warrior' in the place of 'Spanish dancer'.

Dressed in Blue

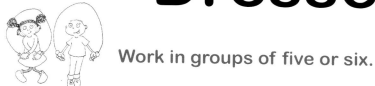

Work in groups of five or six.

Girl guide (airman), girl guide (airman) dressed in blue
↘S   S   S   S

These are the actions you must do.
S   S   S   S

Stand to attention, stand at ease
S   S
├——jump with hands by your side——┤ ├——jump with legs apart——┤

Bend your elbows, bend your knees.
S   S
├——jump and bend your elbows——┤ ├——jump and bend your knees——┤

Salute to the captain, bow to the queen
S   S
├————jump and salute————┤ ├————jump and bow————┤

Turn your back on the submarine.
S   S
├————jump around to face in the opposite direction————┤

I can do heel and toe, I can do the splits
├——hop on one foot touching the heel and toe of the other foot——┤├-stop the rope with your legs astride-┤

I can do the hootchy kootchy, just like this.
├————wiggle hips————┤

Abbreviations

↘S   - child jumps 'in'
S↗   - child jumps 'out'
S   - one skip
Ⓐ   - swing the rope gently from side to side
Ⓑ   - swing the rope in a full circle

25

Captain Cook

Captain Cook lost one arm.

S   S   S   S

├── put one arm behind back ──┤

Captain Cook lost the other arm.

S   S   S   S

├── put the other arm behind back ──┤

Captain Cook lost one eye.

S   S   S   S

├── shut one eye ──┤

Captain Cook lost the other eye.

S   S   S   S

├── shut the other eye ──┤

Captain Cook lost one leg.

S   S   S   S

├── hop on one leg ──┤

Captain Cook lost the other leg.

S   S   S   S↗

├── jump out of the rope ──┤

This is quite a challenging activity and best kept until the children have gained some degree of competence. Also the rope needs to be turned or swung in a very regular rhythm.

Abbreviations

↘S - child jumps 'in'

S↗ - child jumps 'out'

S - one skip

Ⓐ - swing the rope gently from side to side

Ⓑ - swing the rope in a full circle

Skipping Resources

Visit the following web sites to learn more about rope skipping, including news, the rules of the sport, country contacts, skills list, competitions, events, and links to other informative rope-skipping sites.

- The British Heart Foundation (www.bhf.org.uk/youngpeople/index.asp?seco ndlevel=397&thirdlevel=407&artID=676)

- European Rope Skipping Organisation (www.erso.org)

- General (www.directory.webguest.com /Sports/Rope_Skipping)

- British Rope Skipping Association (www.fun-and-fitness.com/fitness-focus)

- International Rope Skipping Federation (www.irsf.org)

Other titles in the Learning Through Action series

Playground Games

By Jenny Mosley and Helen Sonnet, illustrated by Mark Cripps

Lots of children now have no experience of traditional playground games and are missing out on a rich store of imaginative activities. This selection will teach children teamwork, adherence to rules, leader and follower skills and, most importantly, how to have a good time as a collaborative group. Teachers and midday supervisors will love this collection as well!

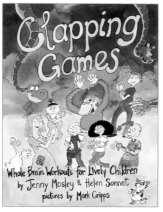

Clapping Games

By Jenny Mosley and Helen Sonnet, illustrated by Mark Cripps

This first collection of clapping games includes old favourites and brand new rhymes. With colourful illustrations and beautiful details, the games in this large format, full-colour book develop listening skills, head and hand coordination, memory, and language skills in a fun and entertaining format. Includes CD.

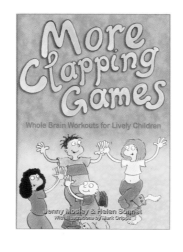

More Clapping Games

By Jenny Mosley and Helen Sonnet, illustrated by Mark Cripps

Building on the success of the first book, this new book expands the repertoire by 30 new clapping games which will appeal to older as well as younger children. Includes a DVD, demonstrating the games as performed by KS1 and KS2 children.

For further details, or to request our Catalogue, please contact:

Positive Press Ltd.
28A Gloucester Rd
Trowbridge, Wiltshire
BA14 0AA
Tel: 01225 767157
Email: positivepress@jennymosley.co.uk
Website: www.circle-time.co.uk.